Dia de los Muertos

Day of the Dead and Sugar Skull Coloring Book

Celebration Edition

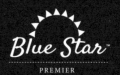

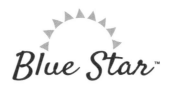

Blue Star™

Teamwork makes the dream work

Design & Production
Chris Ramirez
Tommy Barros
JP Garrigues
Peter Licalzi

Publishing & Ops
Brenna Dominguez
Clare Burch
Kiersten Blair
Reagan Lewis
Camden Hendricks

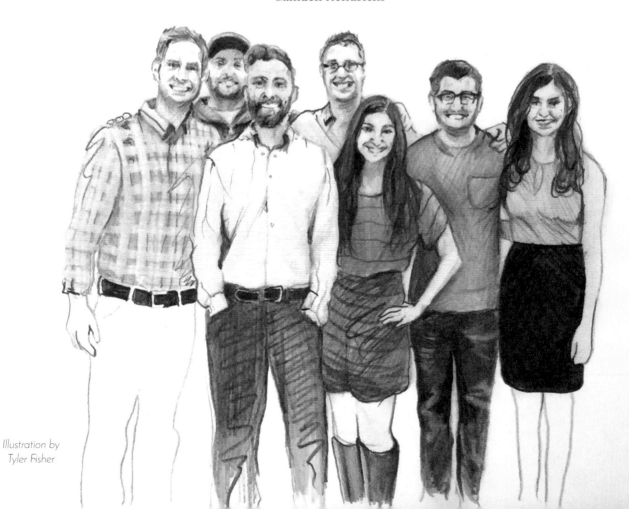

Illustration by
Tyler Fisher

This Book Belongs to

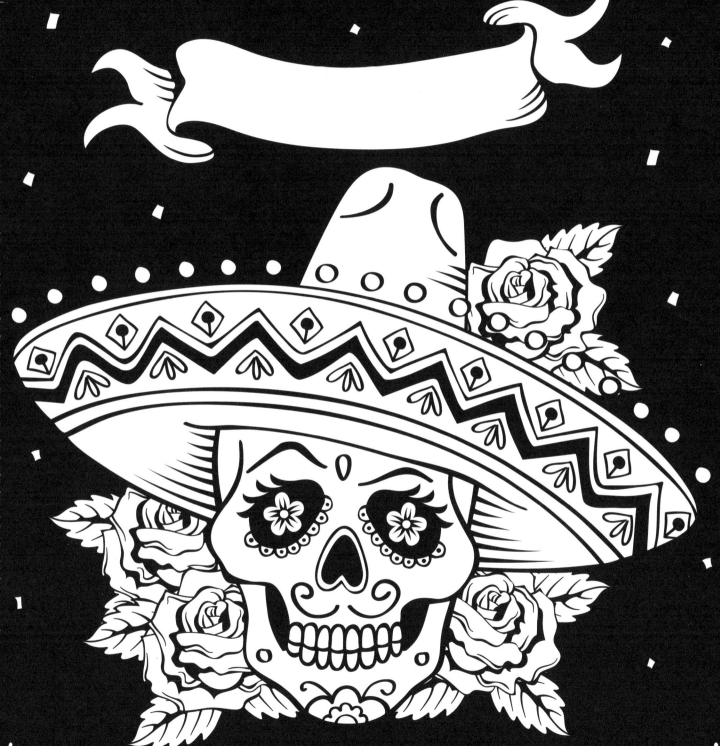

Show us your art...
We'll show the world.

/bluestarcoloring

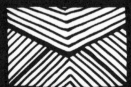
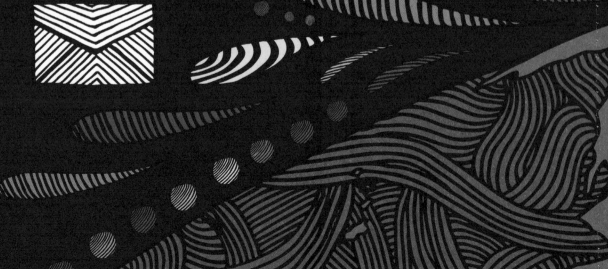

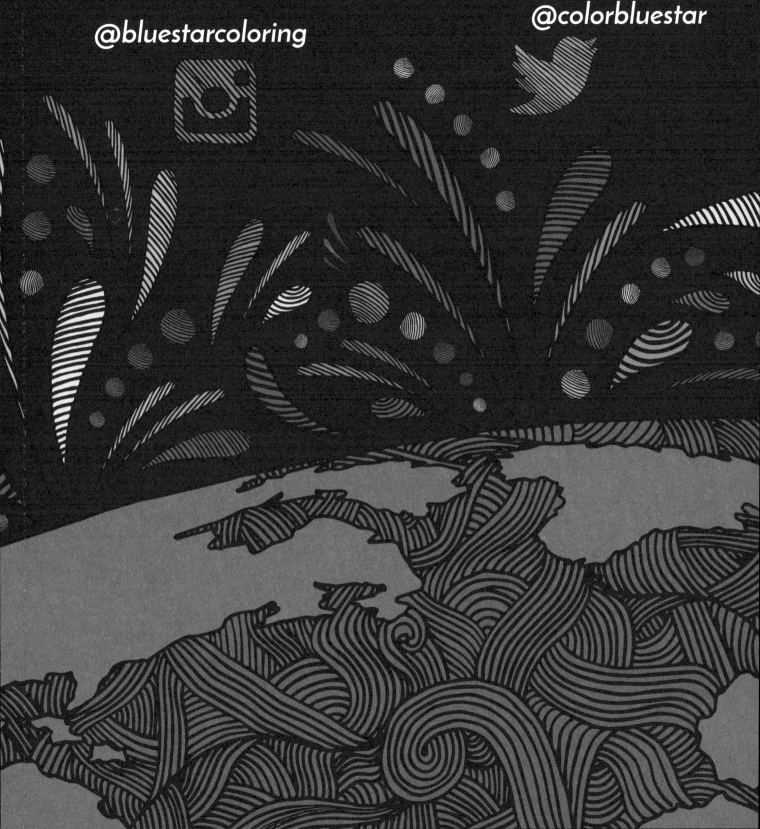

We'll never be perfect, but that won't stop us from trying. Your feedback makes us a better company. We want your ideas, criticism, compliments or anything else you think we should hear! We created the *Celebration Edition* series with YOUR feedback in mind!

Send anything and everything to contact@bluestarcoloring.com.

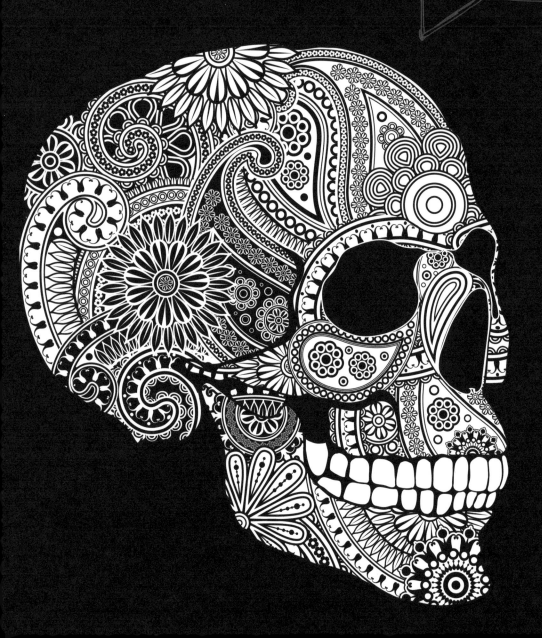

How to Use This Book

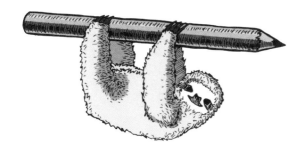

① Break out your crayons or colored pencils.

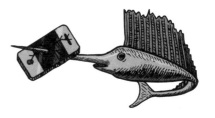

② Turn off your phone, tablet, computer, whatever.

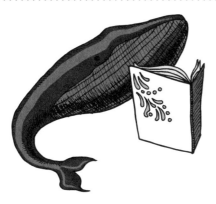

③ Find your favorite page in the book. That is the beginning.

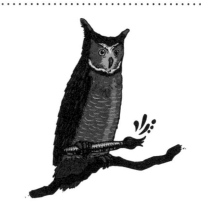

④ Start coloring.

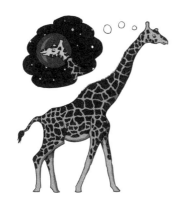

⑤ If you notice at any point that you are forgetting your worries, daydreaming freely or feeling more creative, curious, excitable, delighted, relaxed or any combination thereof, take a deep breath and enjoy it. Remind yourself that coloring, like dancing or falling in love, does not have a point. It is the point.

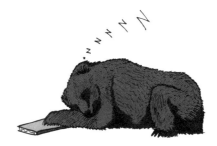

⑥ When you don't feel like it anymore, stop.

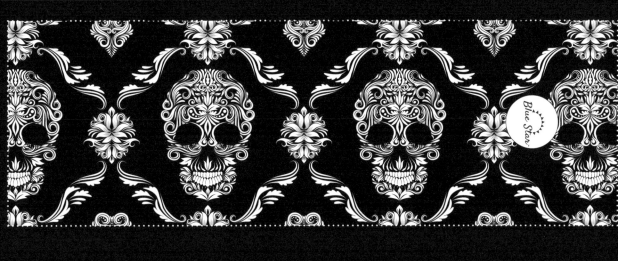

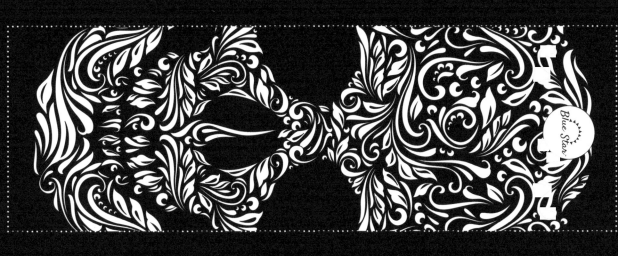

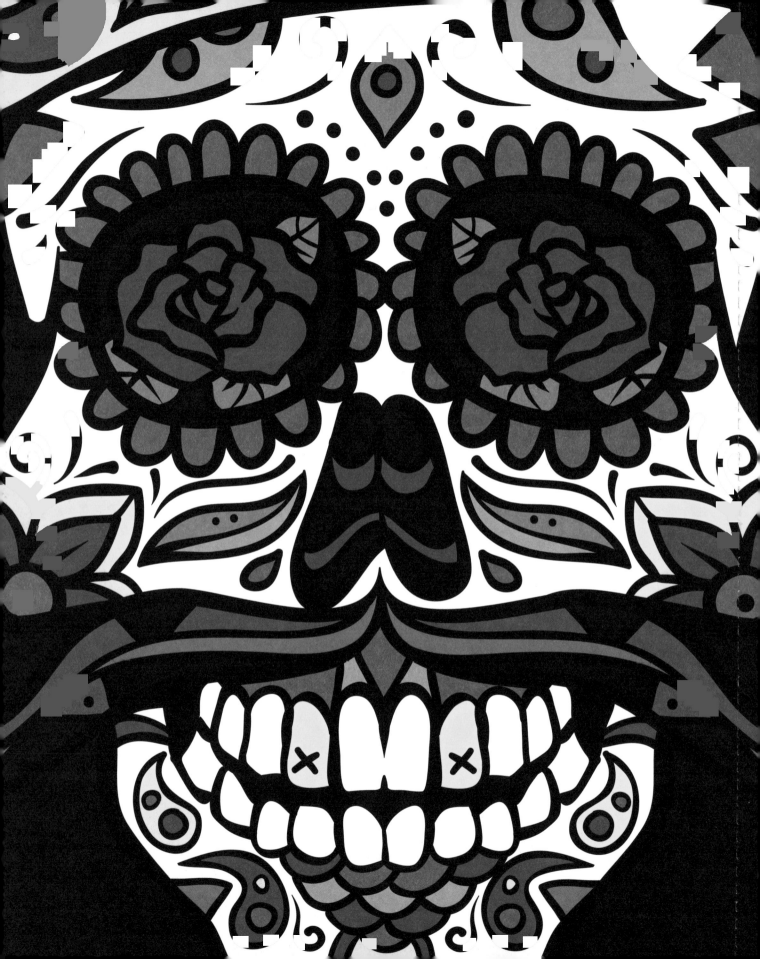

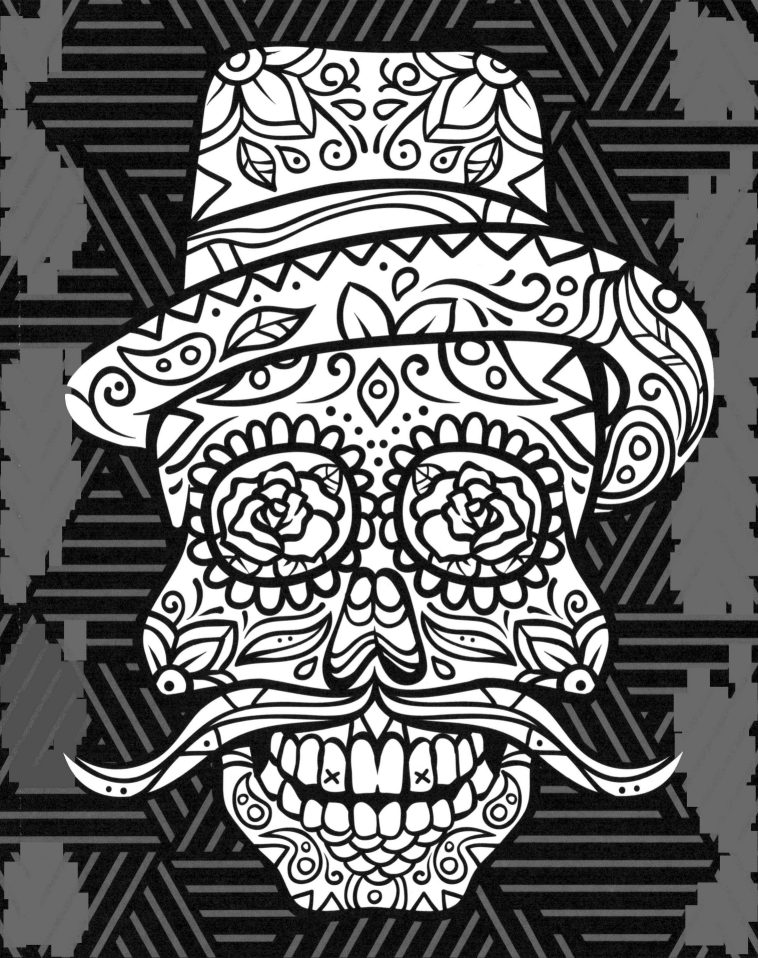

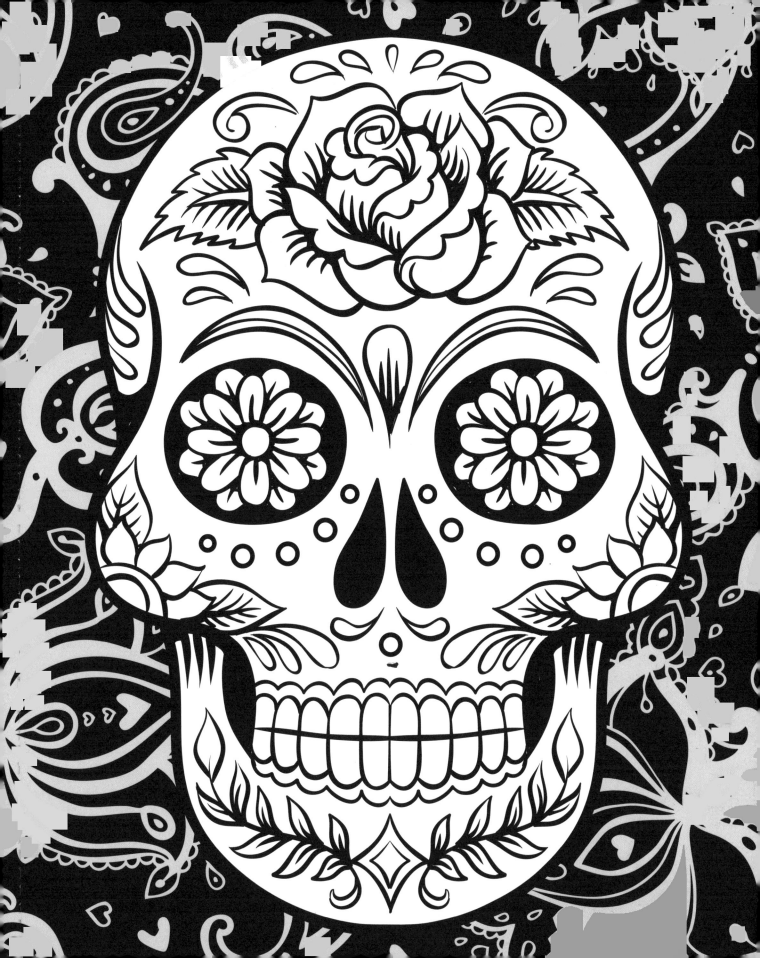

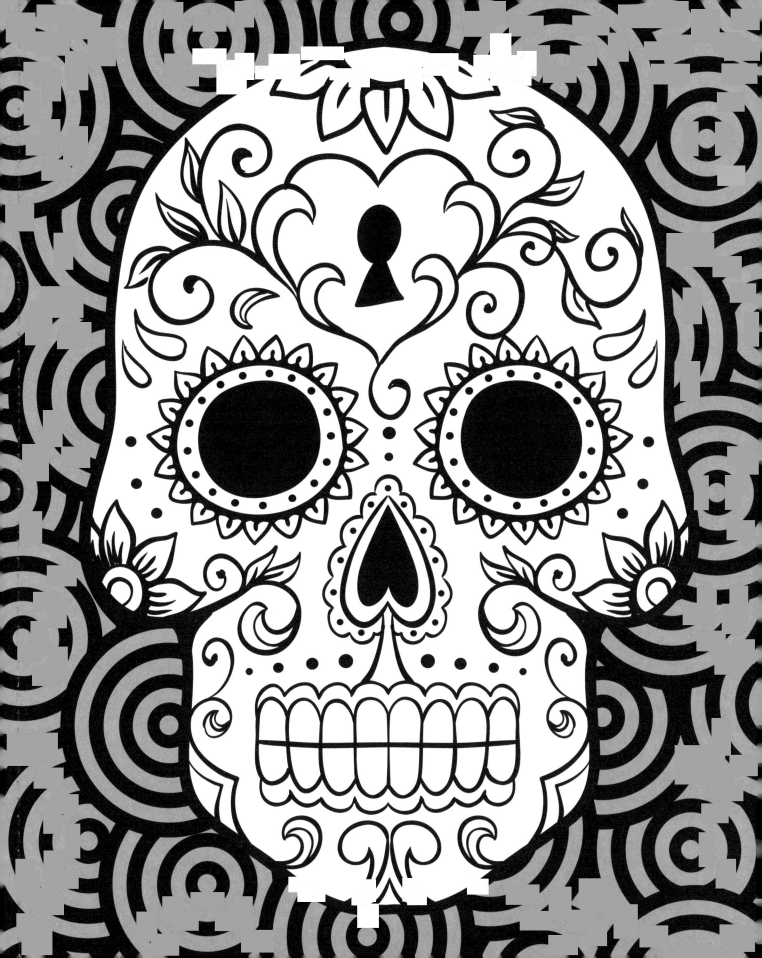

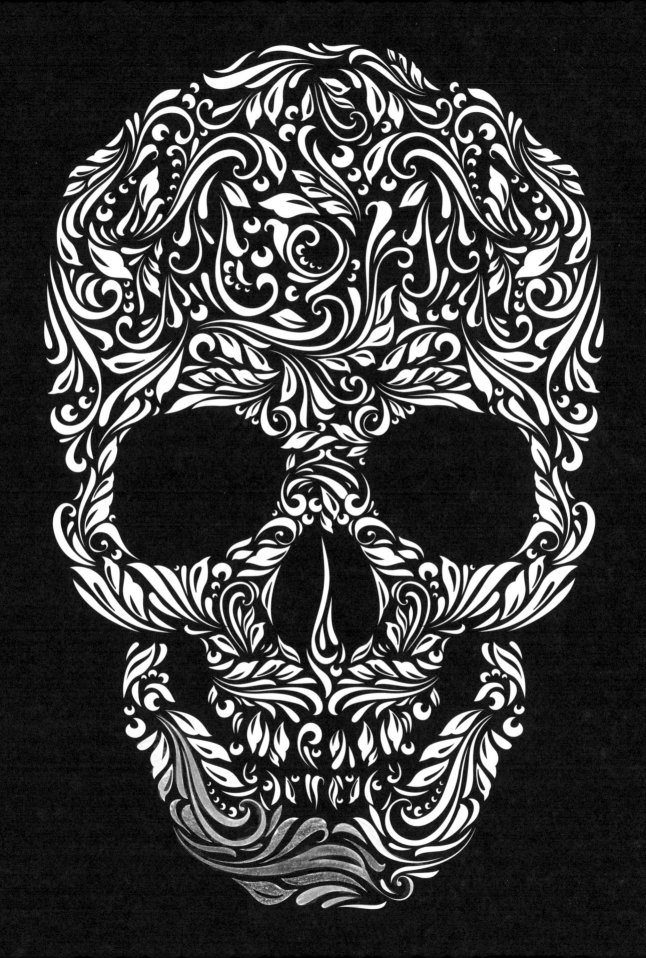

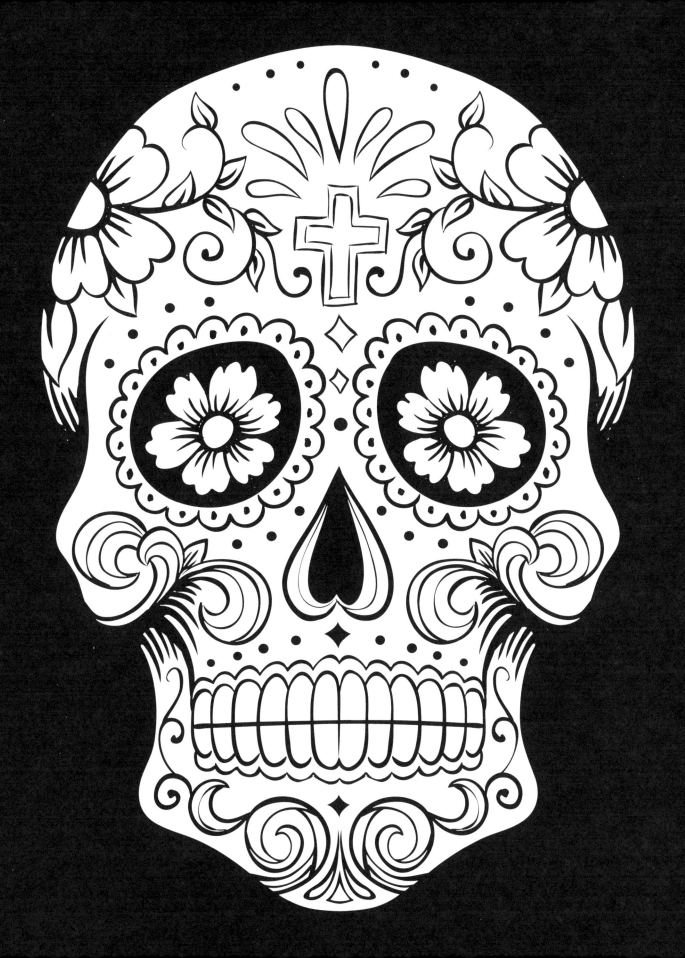

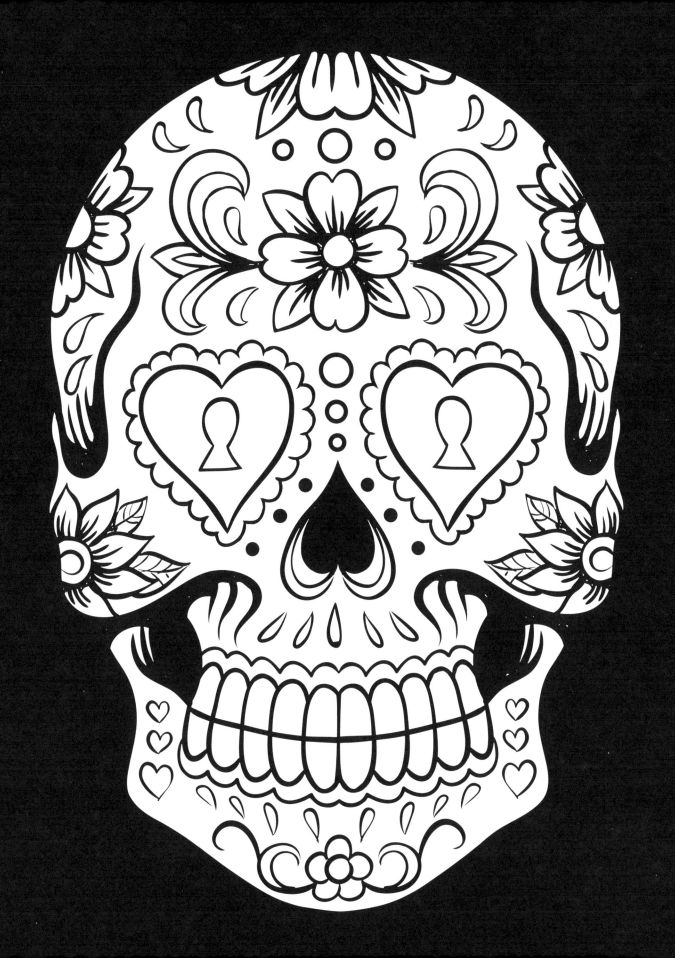

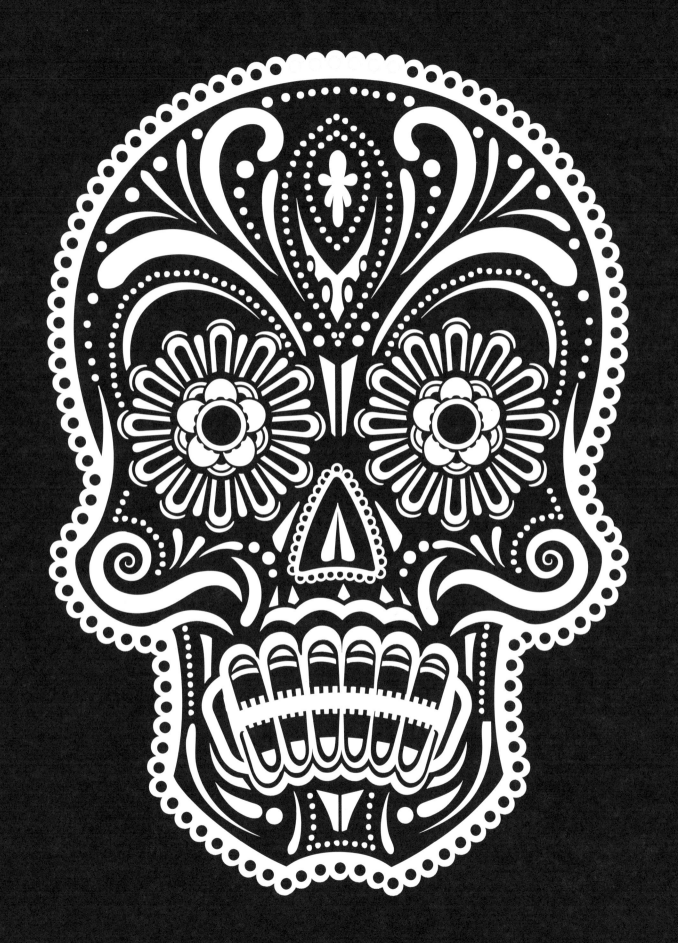

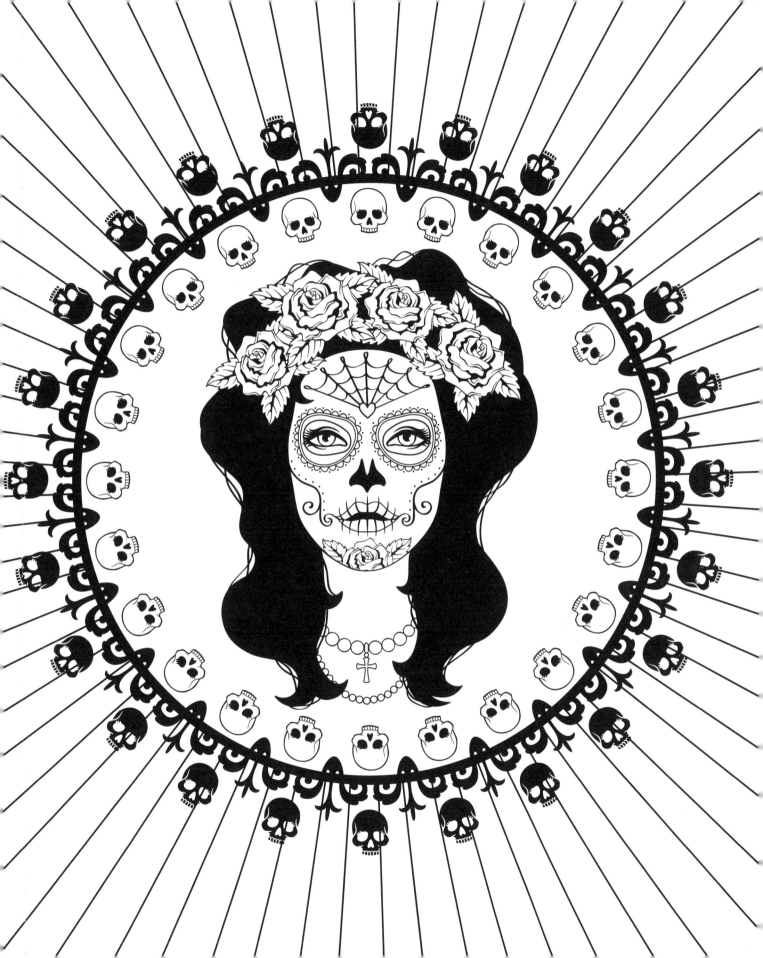

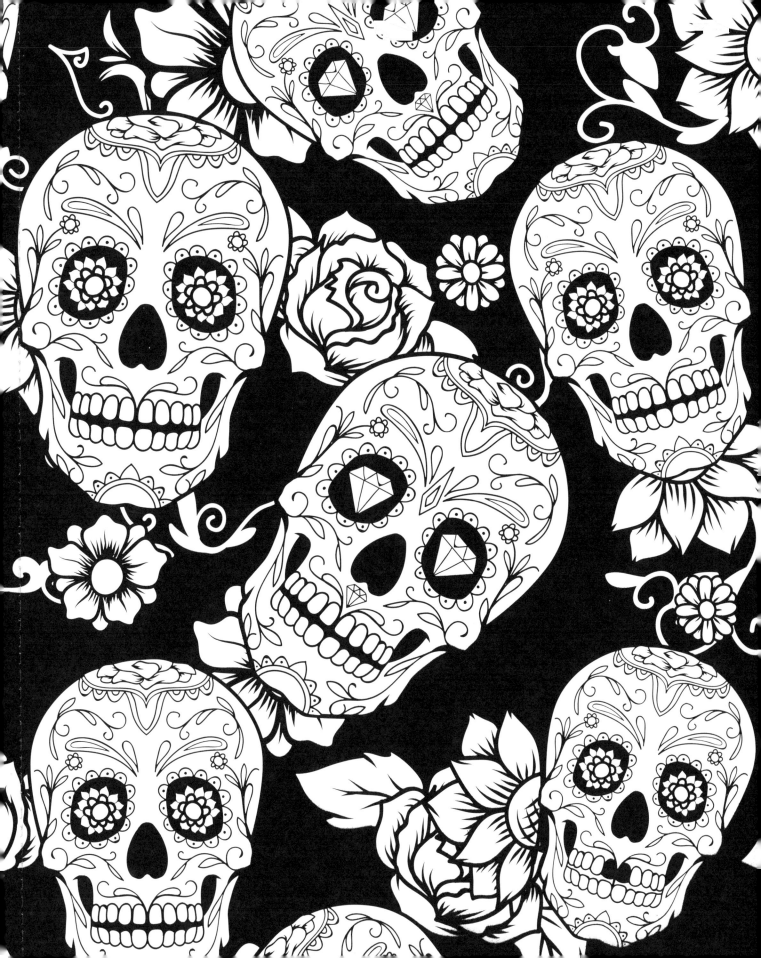

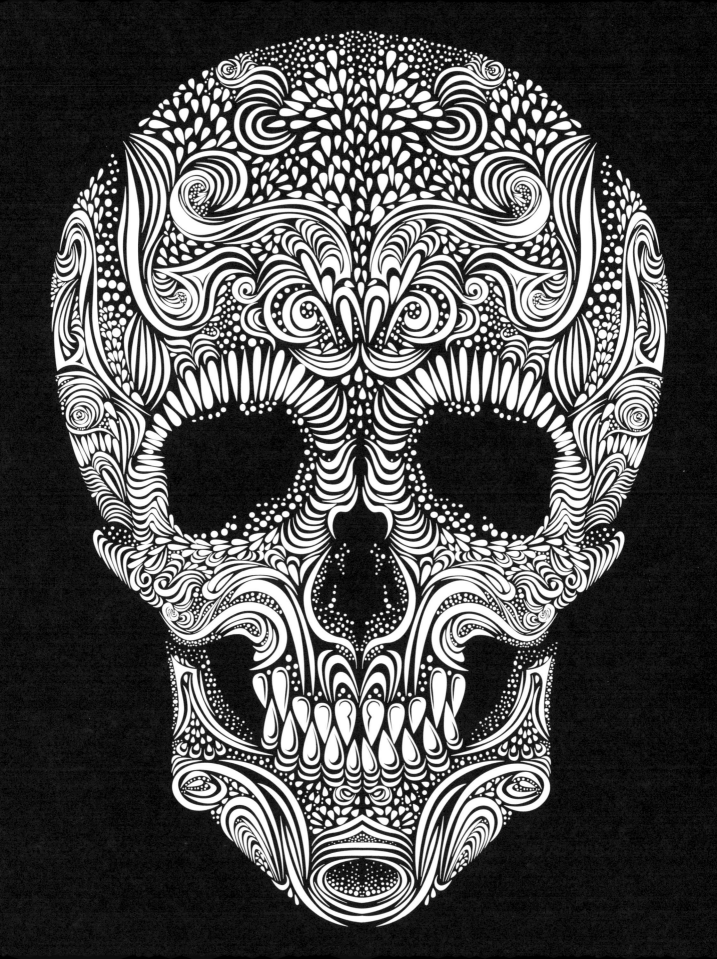

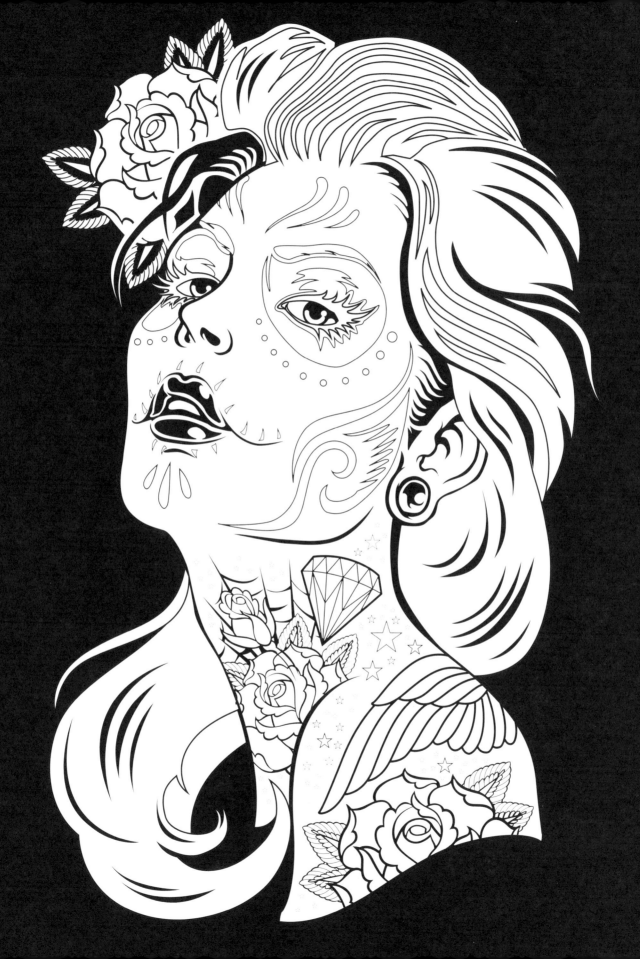

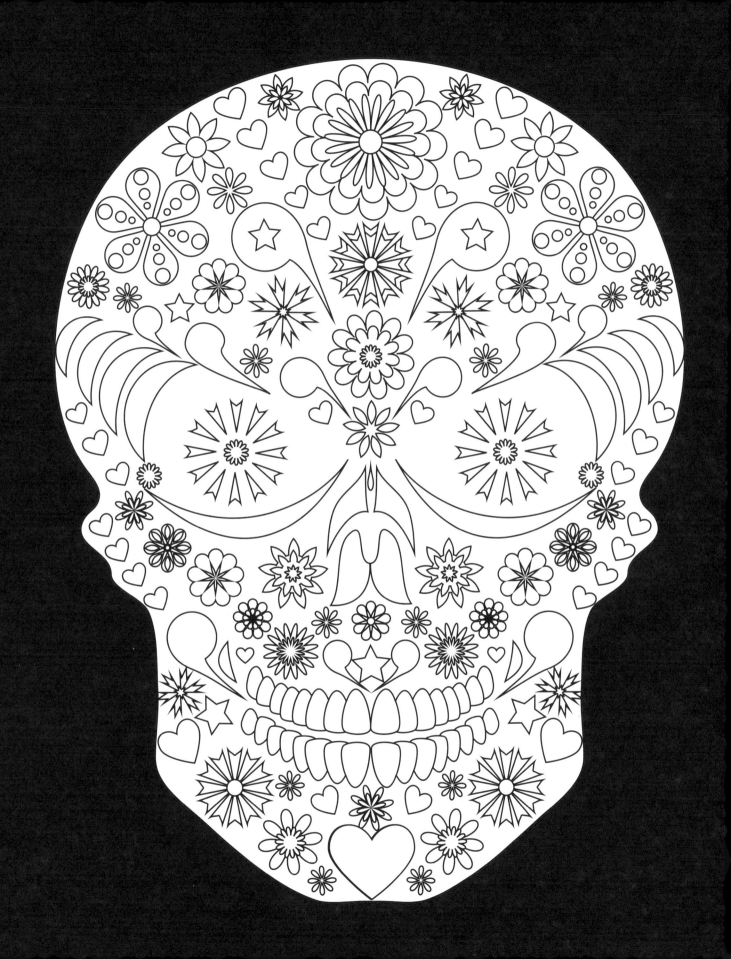

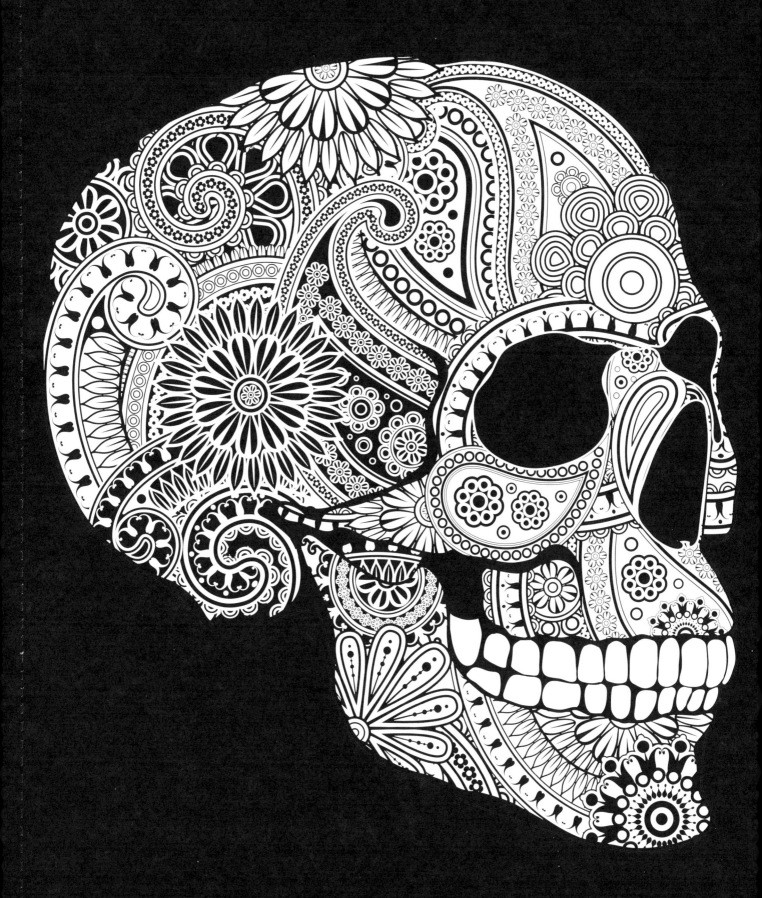

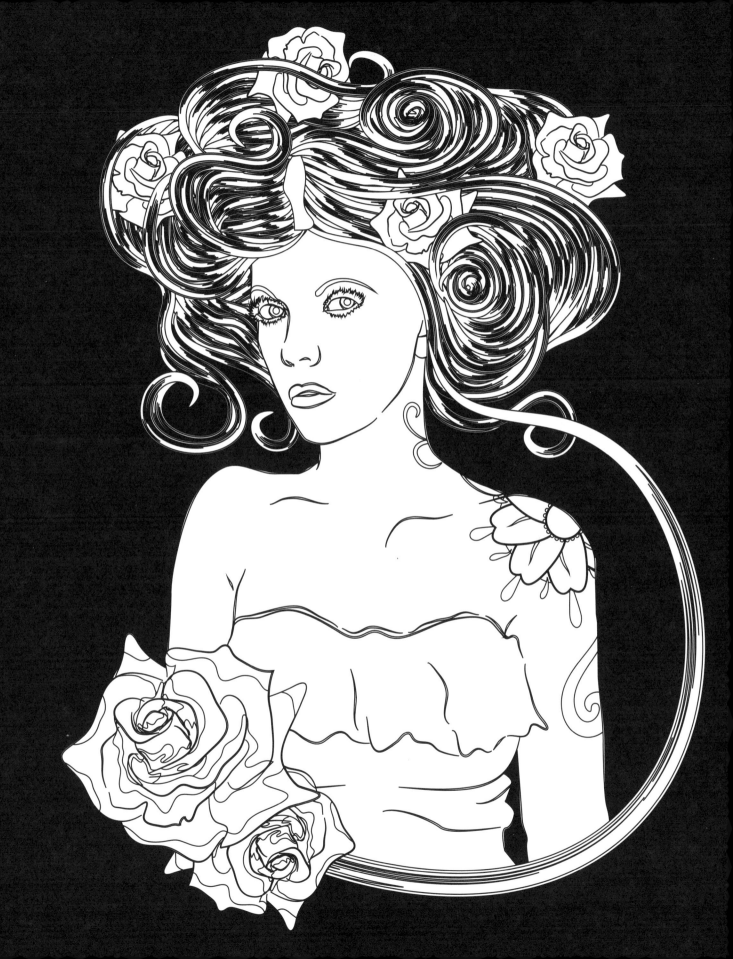

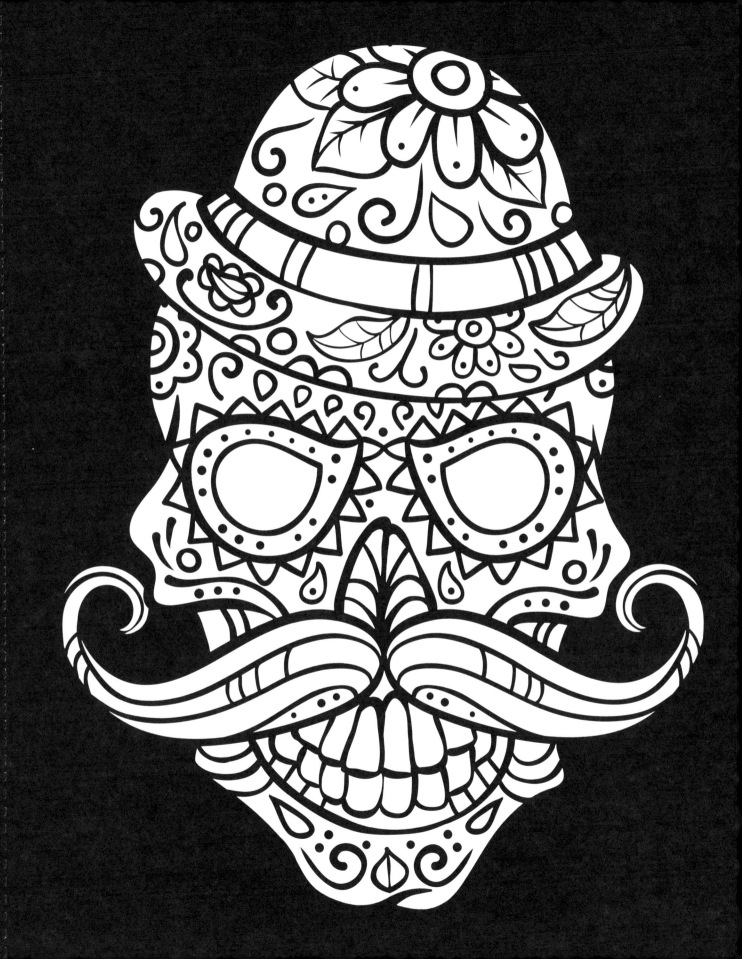

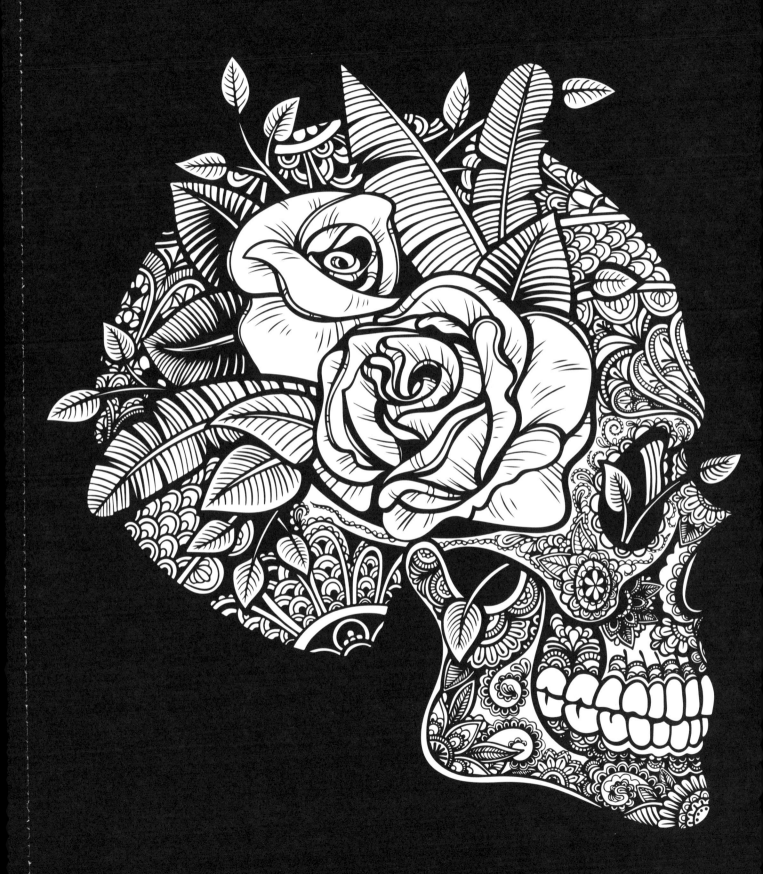

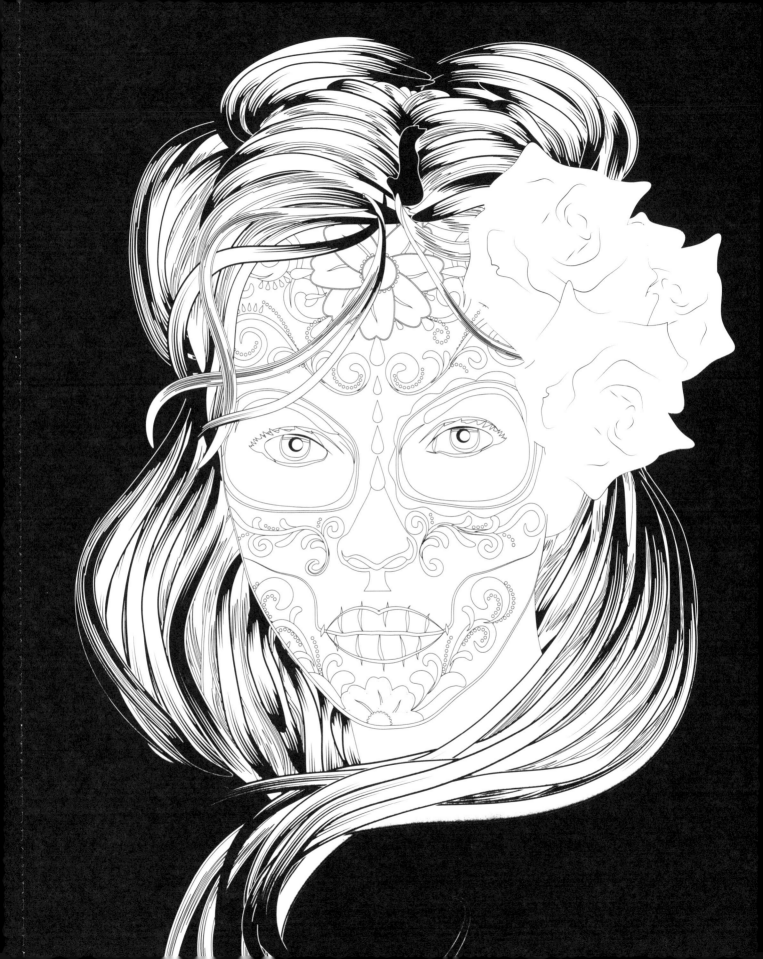

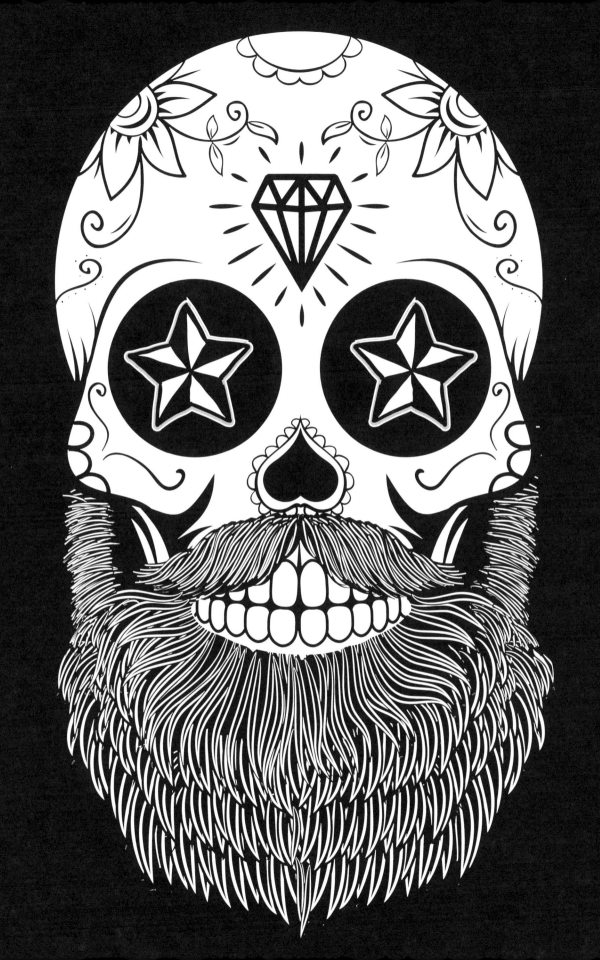

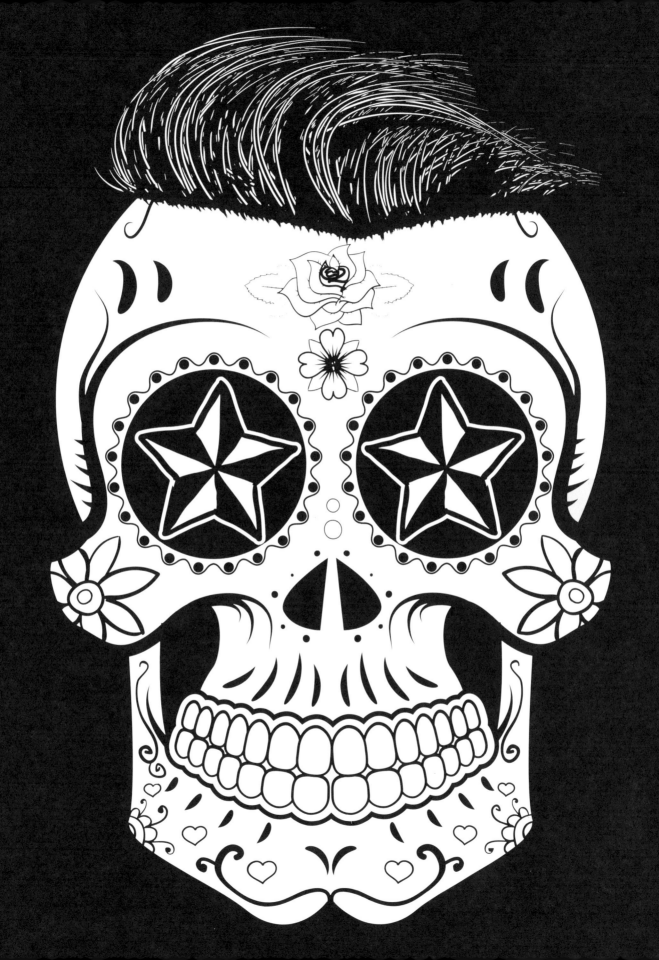

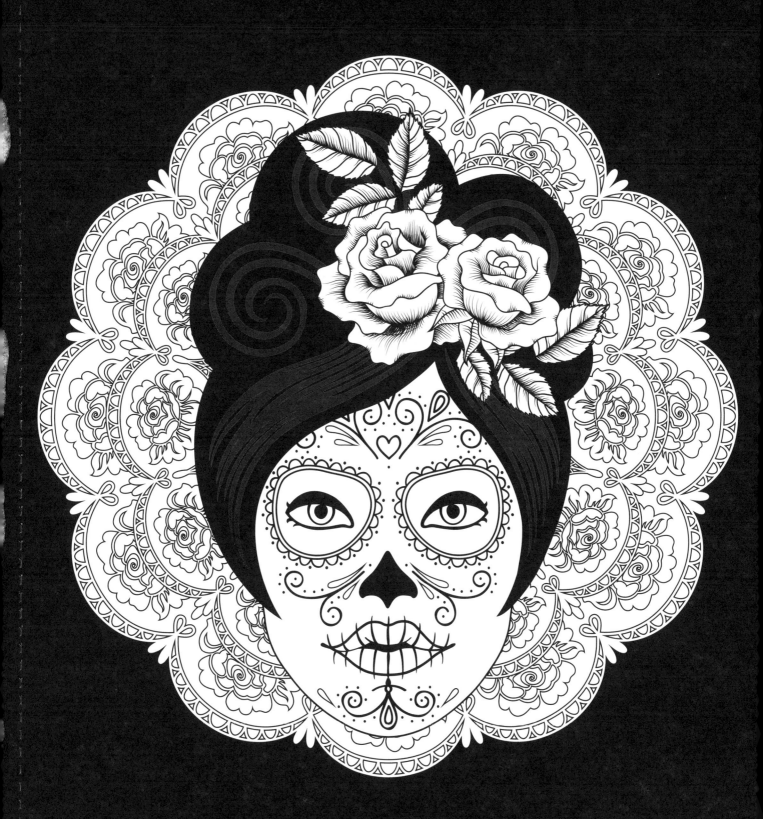

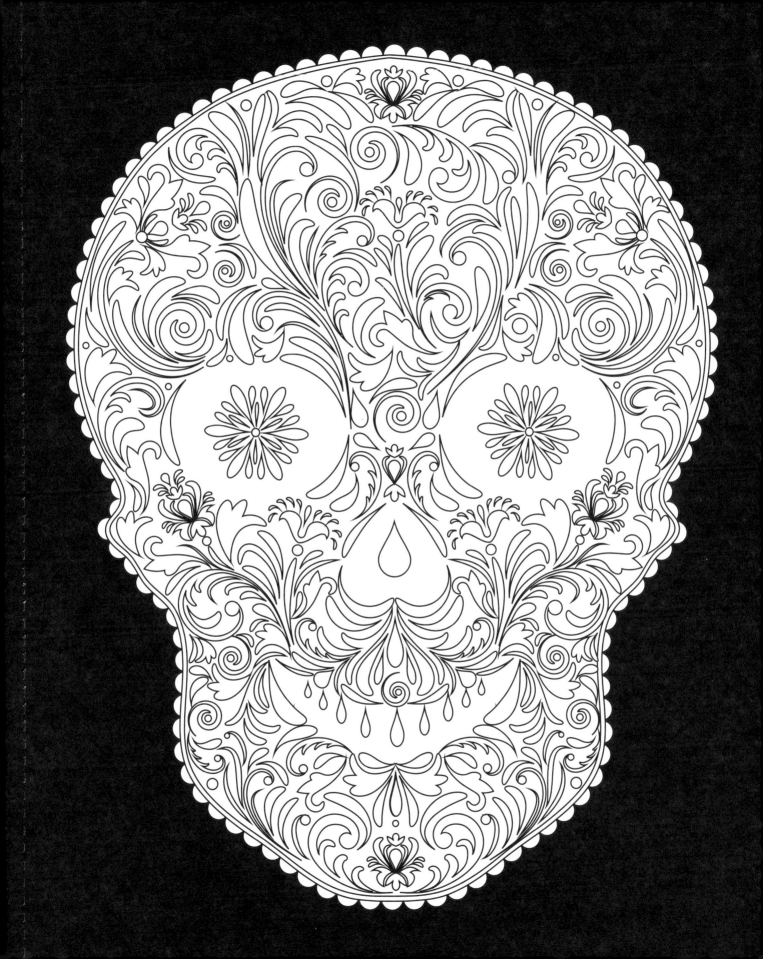

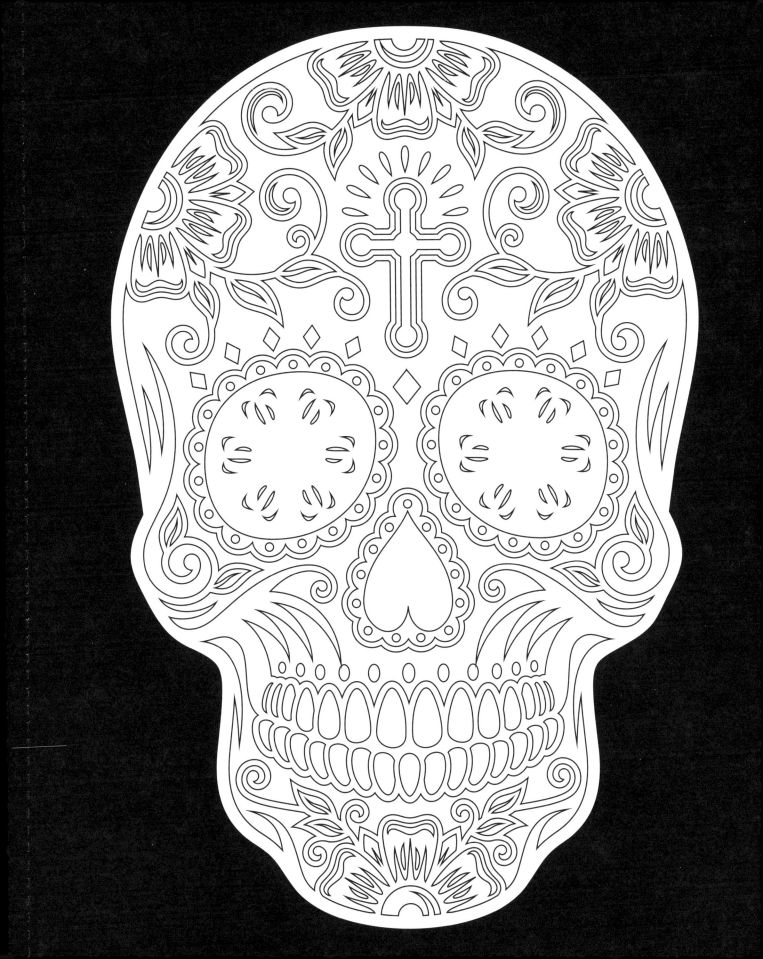

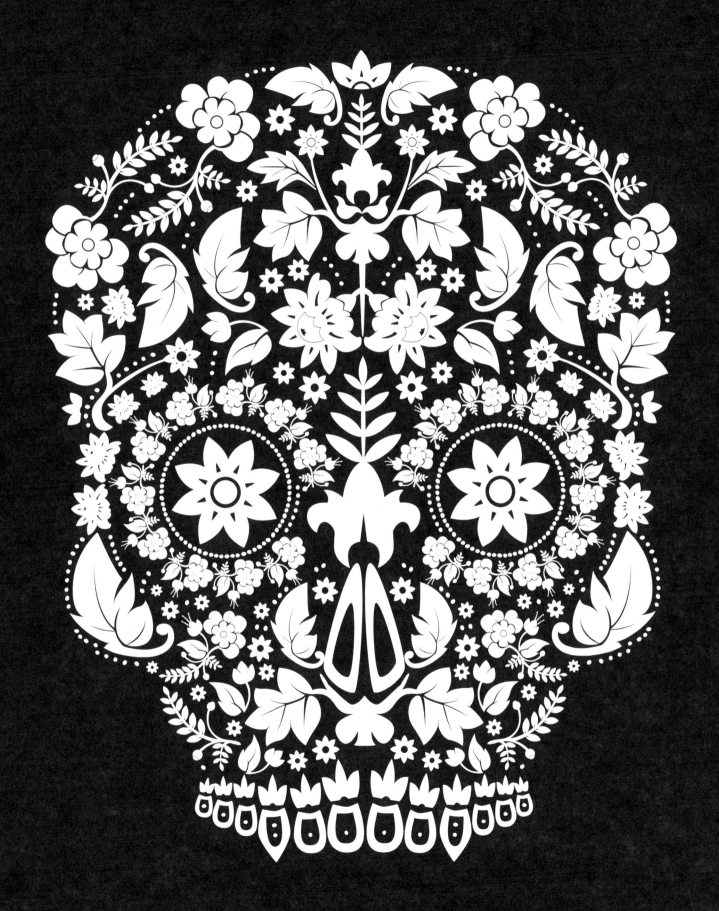

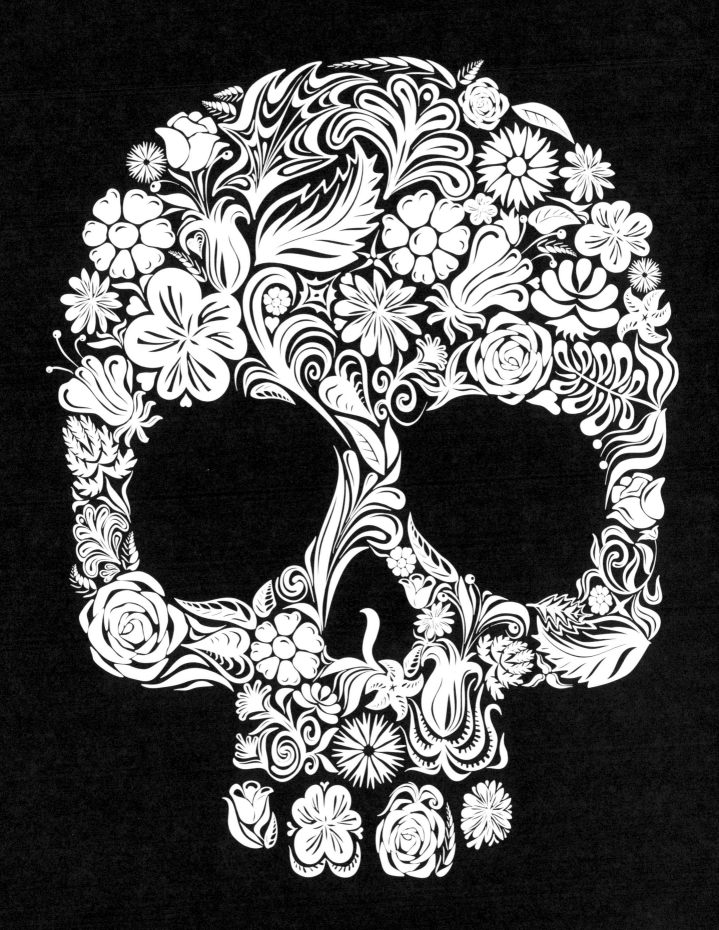

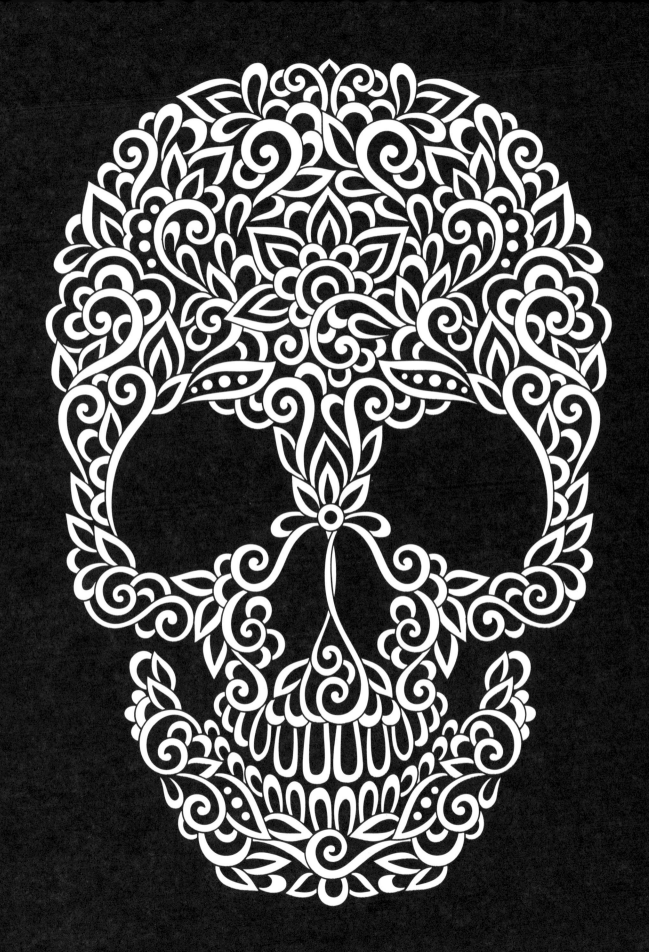

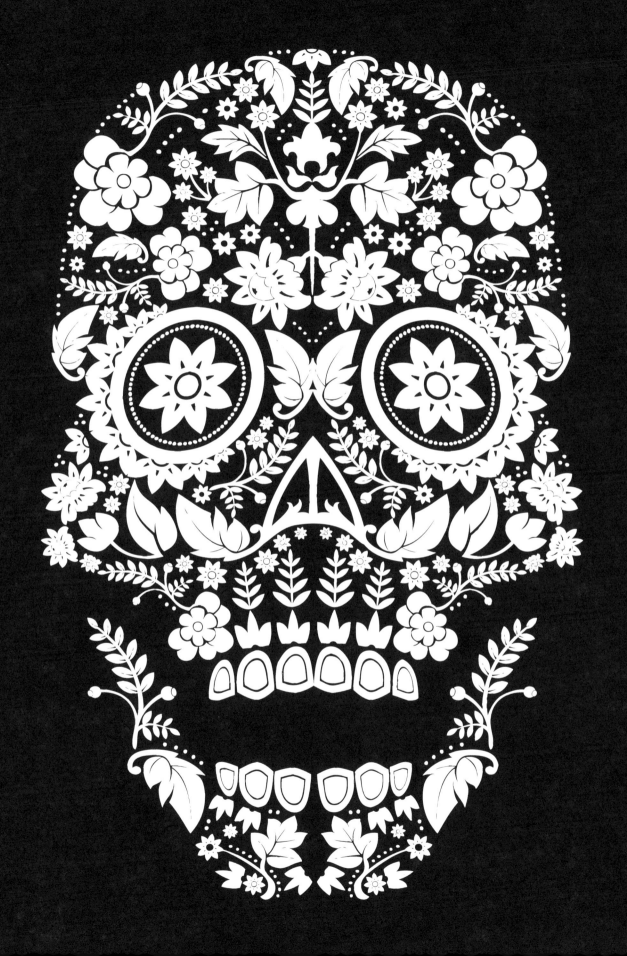

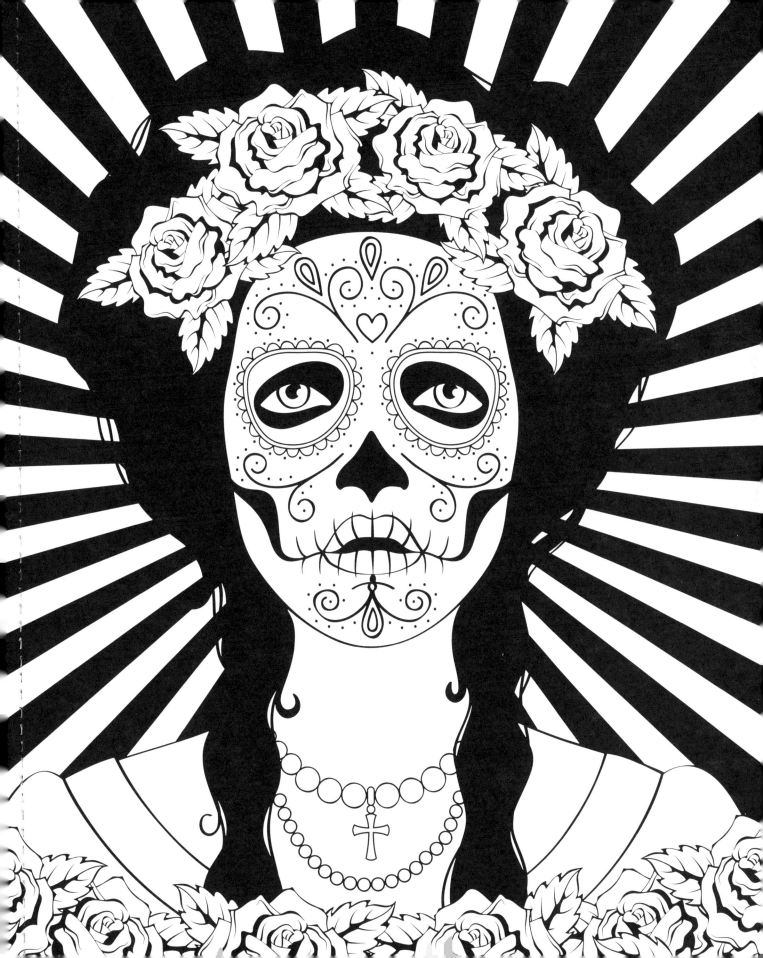

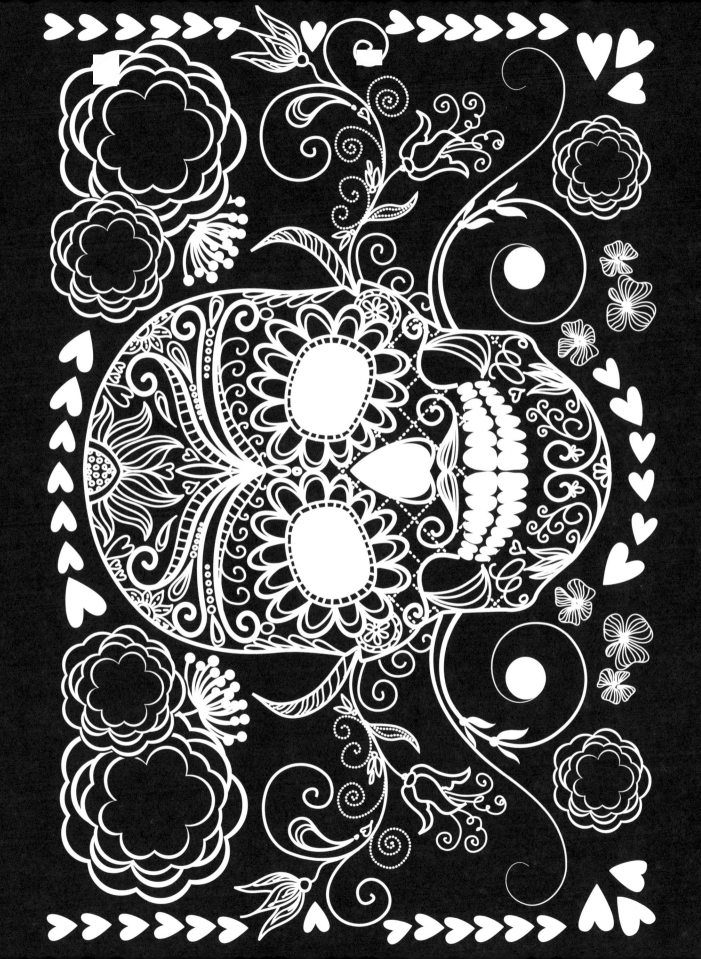

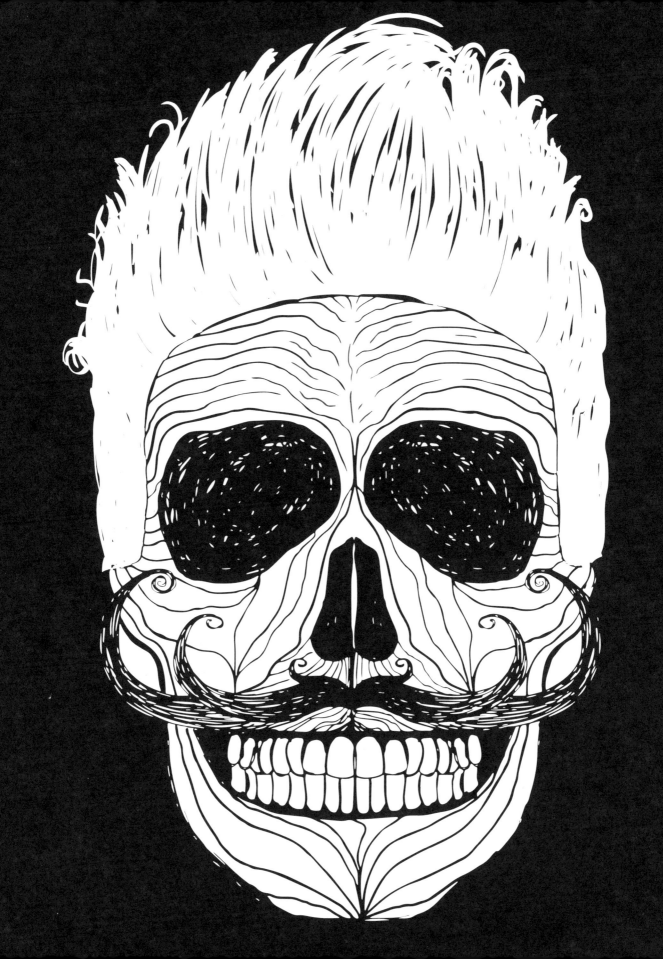

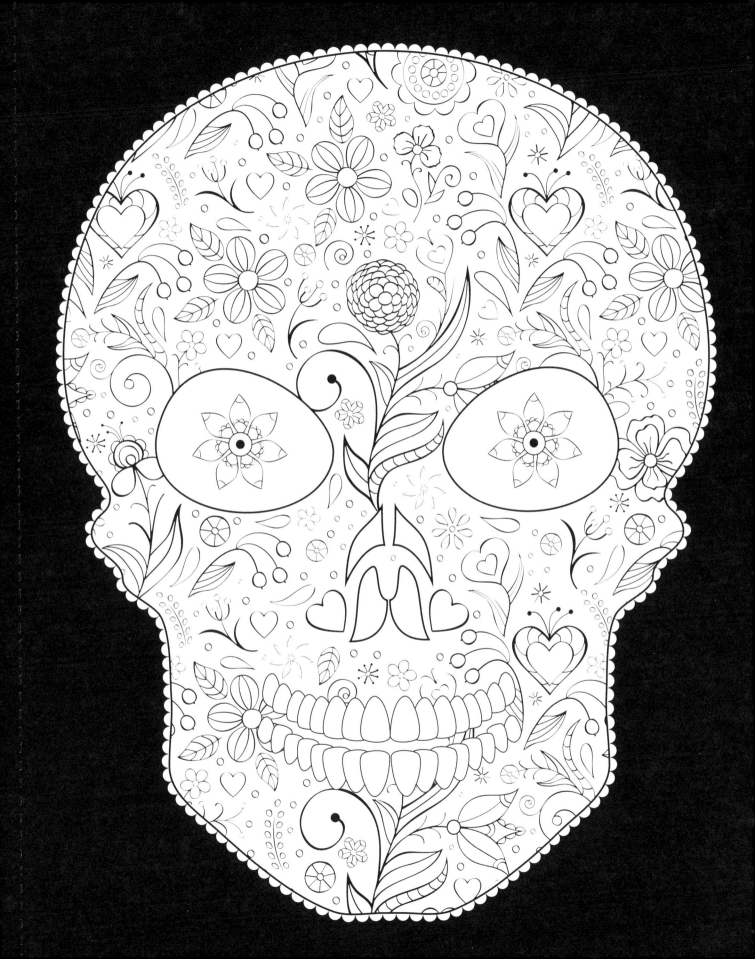

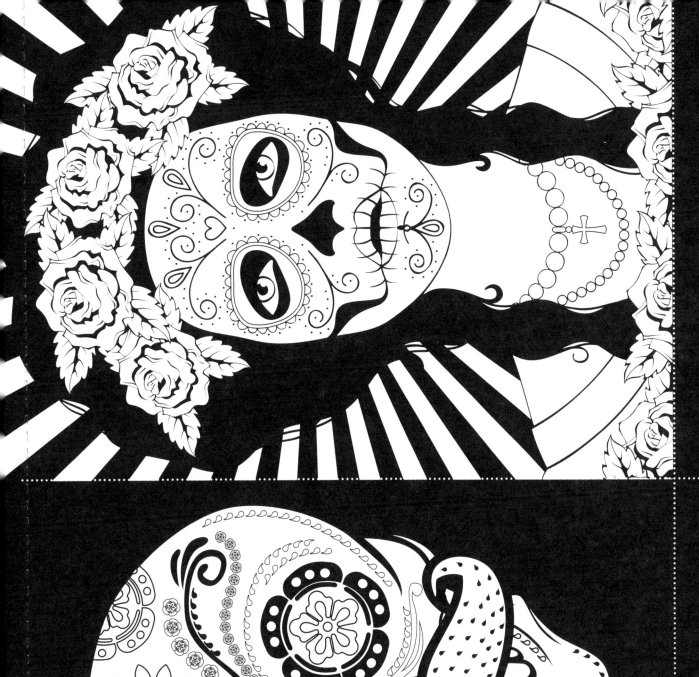
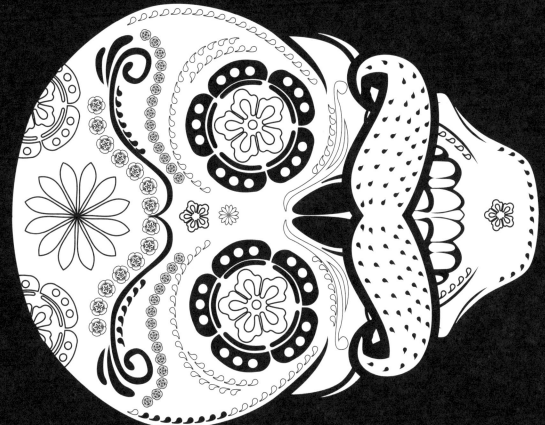

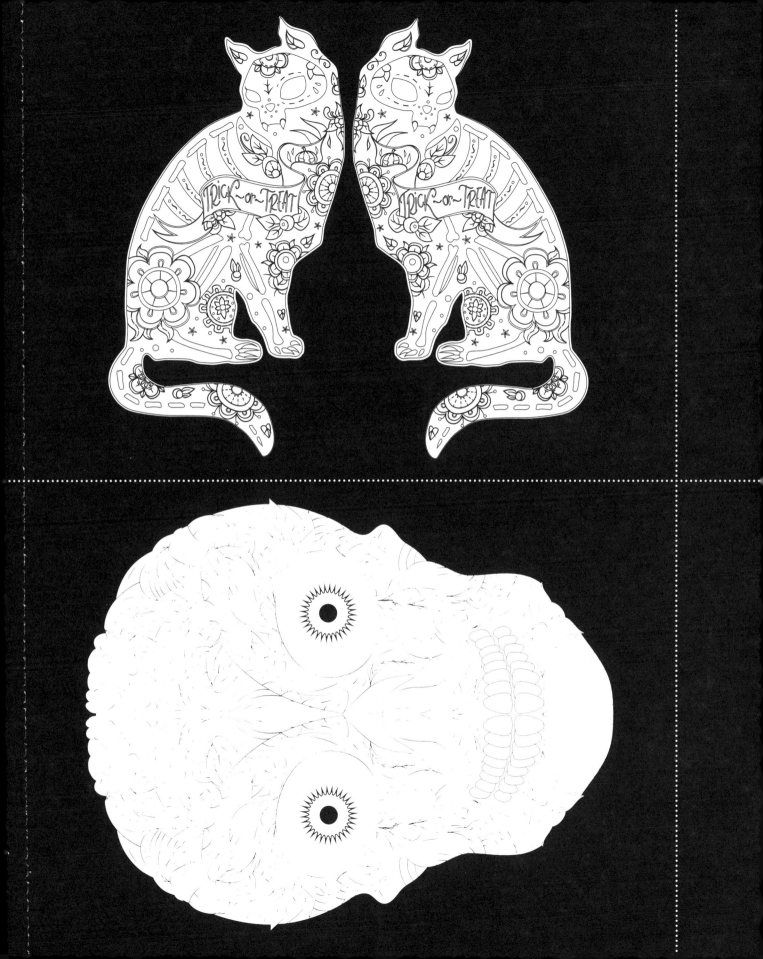

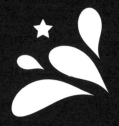
Bonus Image!

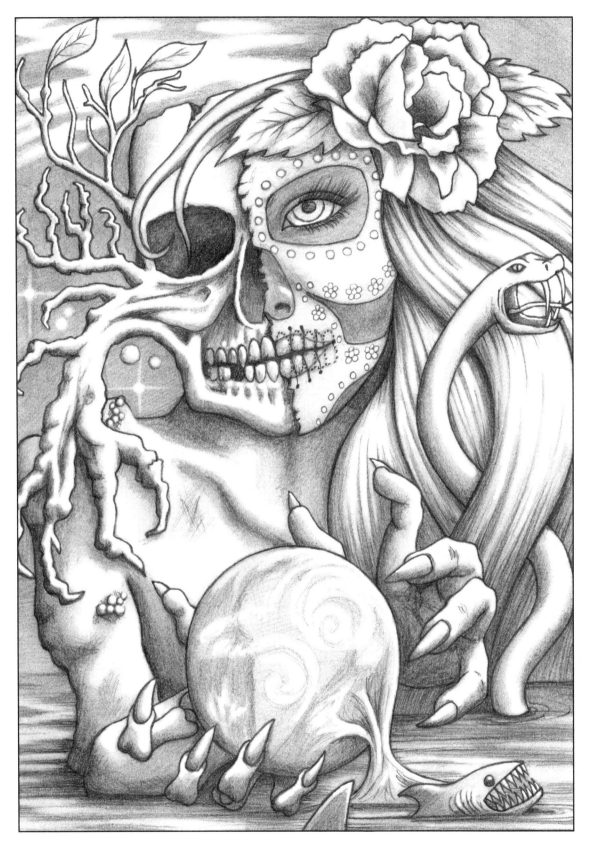

Dark Skies
by Teri Sherman

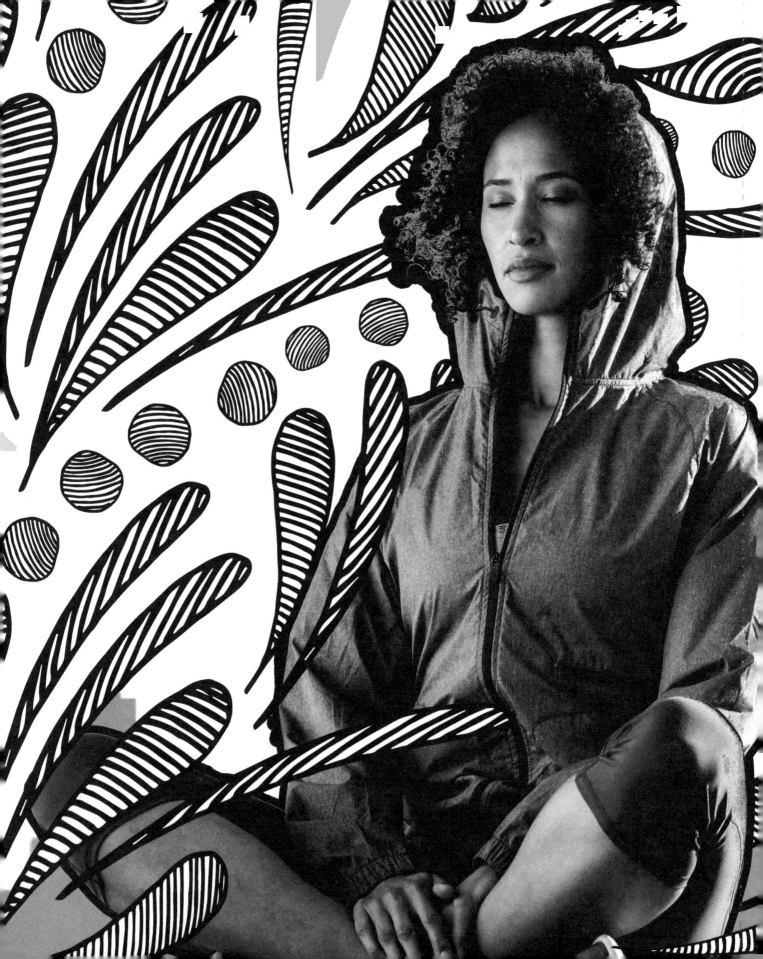

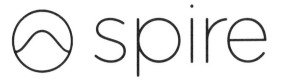

Find Your Calm with Blue Star Coloring + Spire

Discover the mindfulness + activity tracker that helps you be calm – everywhere you go. Blue Star Coloring and Spire have partnered to bring you tranquility in all facets of life. Use Spire to track your state of mind – and when things get a little tense, pick up a Blue Star Coloring book to wind down, refocus, and bring energy back into your day.

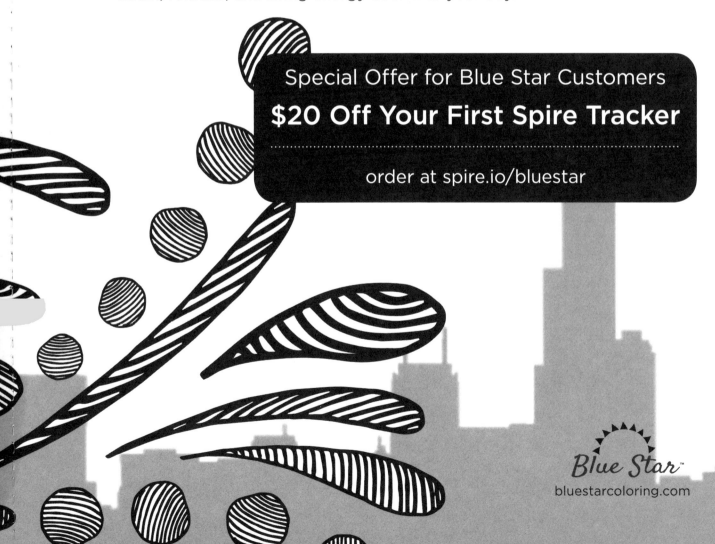

Blue Star™
bluestarcoloring.com